# WEAPONS & WARFARE

BY
JOHN GUY

# Early Weapons & Warfare

T he need for fortification has been with us since men and women began living in towns. Urban life, since 7000 B.C., gave birth to private property and the need to defend it from outsiders. That need has been with us ever since and seems likely to remain so. In the same way the primitive weapons that had been devised purely for hunting came to have a dual purpose: they began to be used to injure and kill *people*. The ingenuity with which humans have devoted their skills to destroying their own kind is a sad reflection on our species. No other animal expends such energy in pursuit of killing.

### BRONZE AGE SHIELDS

Tribal leaders in Bronze Age Europe (c. 2000 B.C.– c. 600 B.C.) decorated both their weapons and their armor to display their position in the community. This magnificent bronze shield dates from the 1st century A.D. and was discovered at Battersea, in London, preserved in the mud of the Thames River. Made from bronze and gold and decorated with red glass studs (then a valuable material), the raised patterns were fashioned by hammering from the reverse side.

### THE AGE OF METAL

Prior to c. 2500 B.C. most tools and weapons were fashioned from stone. Hammers and maces were made by simply lashing a shaped stone to a wooden handle, while sharp flints, shaped to a point, made ideal spearheads and arrowheads. At about that time, however, the technique of manufacturing metals from natural ores developed. This hard-edged, bronze dagger (made from pouring liquid tin and coppe into a mold) revolutionized weapon design.

### THE MACE

Along with the spear, the mace is one of the earliest weapons used by man. In prehistoric times clubs were probably fashioned from the thigh bones of animals or from hard, knobbly wood. The mace is a direct derivative of the simple club. By medieval times it had been fashioned into a formidable weapon, with the rounded end made of flanged metal and often reinforced with studs or spikes to pierce metal armor and inflict horrible injuries.

## HILL FORTS

From about 1000 B.C. a type of fortification known as hill forts began to appear in Britain. They remained in use throughout the Iron Age until the Roman occupation. They were large communal, defensive enclosures. They consisted usually of a large, levelled enclosure on top of a hill, surrounded by one or more massive earthen ramparts, usually surmounted by timber palisades or stone walls.

## BROCHS & DUNS

About 200 B.C. another type of fortification, known as brochs and duns, began to appear in Iron Age Britain, principally in Scotland. They were hollow stone towers, about 40–50 ft. high, usually circular or D-shaped, with timber buildings arranged around a central courtyard. Unlike hill forts, which were communal defenses, these towers were the fortified farmhouses of a single family or small group of people. The impressive example shown here is at Furness, in the Orkney Isles.

## THE ORIENT

In the West, an important purpose of armor (other than to offer its wearer protection) was to impress onlookers with its finery and craftsmanship. By contrast, the primary objective of this frightening Japanese mask was to intimidate and terrify the enemy—an early form of psychological warfare.

## THE BIBLE AS HISTORY

This picture shows Joshua (chosen by Moses to lead the Israelites) defeating their opponents at Jericho. It is typical of many Biblical stories, which can be viewed as a collection of early historical writings, giving valuable insights into Hebrew history.

# Warfare in the Ancient World

**A**lthough humans have probably always made weapons and waged war against each other, it was the introduction of metal that revolutionized warfare. Swords were not very effective when only flint was available for making a blade—the weapon would have been too fragile and too heavy. The first swords in southwest Asia were made of copper but were too soft and could not hold an edge. They became more effective after the introduction of tin (about 2800 B.C.), which was used to make bronze, a hard metal that retained its cutting edge and was relatively easy to make. Although the Bronze Age is commonly held to have given way to the Iron Age at about 800 B.C., in reality there was considerable overlap. Bronze was manufactured for weapons well into the Iron Age and iron was smelted as early as c. 2700 B.C. in Anatolia. Iron only gradually superseded bronze as the favorite material of weapons.

## THE ROMANS

The emergence of Rome as the dominant city-state in the classical world owed much to the ancient Greeks and the Etruscans, who came from Anatolia (or perhaps the Orient), establishing a number of self-governing city-states. The Romans quickly established a well-trained and well-equipped army that became the most efficient military force then known. A typical Roman legionnaire was equipped with a helmet, an oblong shield, a short sword, and breastplate armor comprised of overlapping metal plates laced together, a type favored by oriental armorers.

## THE GREEKS

The ancient Greek army was largely a civilian force, each soldier supplying his own equipment so that the richest civilians became the best-equipped and most powerful cavalrymen. A typical infantryman (known as a hoplite) was equipped with a bronze helmet (such as this Corinthian example shown to the left, of c. 500 B.C.) and a circular shield. Some soldiers carried short, bronze swords, but the usual weapon was a spear. The favored method of attack was a massed assault by spearsmen to push an enemy back.

## CHARIOTS

Horse-drawn war chariots seem to have originated in southwest Asia, possibly in Iran about 1700 B.C. When the Egyptians extended their empire north, into Anatolia, they brought back chariots and developed them into fast, lightweight fighting platforms. Chariots usually carried two men (one to control the horses and one to fight) and were employed throughout the ancient world after 1700 B.C. The example shown here comes from ancient Sumer.

## THE SIEGE OF TROY

According to Homer, in about 1184 B.C. Helen, wife of Menelaus, King of Sparta, was captured by the Trojans (Troy was a city-state in what is now part of Turkey). Menelaus's brother, Agamemnon, King of Mycenae, united the Greeks and attacked the city of Troy, but after 10 years was unable to capture it. Later legends claimed that the Greeks built a huge wooden horse, supposedly as a gift to the Trojans, and departed. Soldiers, hidden inside the horse, had secretly opened the city gates to let in the returning Greek army, who then destroyed the city.

## GREEK FIRE

"Greek Fire" was an early form of incendiary device employed by Byzantine Greeks and remained in use, in differing forms, but was kept a secret for many years. It is made from a compound of naphtha, saltpeter, and sulfur, contained within earthenware pots, which were then set on fire and hurled at the enemy by the use of catapults. Because of the ingredients used, the flames would burn in water and so became a favorite weapon to use against an enemy's ships.

## THE HITTITES

The Hittites (or "sons of Heth") were a warlike people who occupied a large territory in what is now part of modern-day central Turkey. Their lands bordered the Mitanni (now part of eastern Anatolia) and Egypt. The Hittites were the first people to smelt iron extensively (from about 1400 B.C.) and their use of strong iron swords was probably instrumental in extending their empire over much of southwest Asia.

## ARMORED KNIGHTS

Throughout Europe the development of arms and armor followed much the same pattern and flourished with the development of the feudal system. As the feudal system of government subsided, so the methods of warfare changed and the need for armor declined. In the 11th century, armor consisted principally of a helmet and chain-mail tunic, made up of interconnecting metal rings. Because knights (and all soldiers) were expected to supply their own weapons and armor as part of their feudal service, the more wealthy could afford elaborate suits of plate armor, as shown here. Armor became so heavy and ponderous by the end of the medieval period that it hampered fighting; with the advent of gunpowder it gradually came to be used more for ceremonial occasions than for war.

## TACTICAL SUPREMACY

Toward the end of the European medieval period (from about the mid-14th century on) the tactics of warfare began to change. The emphasis shifted away from attacking and defending castles, once considered the most important of strategies, to open warfare in the field. By this time armies consisted mostly of mercenaries rather than the untrained soldiers provided by the feudal system. At the Battle of Agincourt in 1415, during the 100 Years' War with France, England won a resounding victory against the superior forces of France by the tactical use of archers.

## JAVANESE KRIS

This highly ornate sword, with its wavy blade, comes from Java and is typical of many Indonesian and southeast Asian swords. Known as a "kris," its use was mainly ceremonial, though it was also used in combat. Decorated with gold, silver, and ivory, the blade was usually made of iron, which was then treated with acid to create decorative patterns.

## CHIVALRIC CODE

Its very strict chivalric code belied the often barbaric nature of medieval warfare. Battles would often be decided by negotiation rather than by fighting, or champions might be called upon to decide the outcome, each side selecting a single combatant, or group of knights, to fight on its behalf. If captured, knights were not usually killed, but held for ransom. Nevertheless, injuries inflicted on the battlefield were quite serious, many soldiers dying from secondary infections rather than their wounds.

# Medieval Weapons & Warfare

The period in history known as the Middle Ages was, for many parts of the world, an era of great upheaval. In Europe particularly, great power struggles were waged between lords and kings in their thirst for land and prestige. Many of today's political boundaries were established at this time. Europe and Japan were dominated by the feudal system, or variations of it, in which kings ultimately owned all the land in their kingdom, which they let out to various lords. They in turn let out their land to sub-tenants, lesser barons, or knights. The result was a continuous struggle for power and supremacy either between the king and his barons or between the barons themselves as they jostled for position.

## THE VIKINGS

Contrary to popular belief, the Vikings did not usually wear horned helmets, though some leaders may have worn them on ceremonial occasions. A typical Viking warrior wore a helmet, sometimes with terrifying face mask (such as the one shown here), a tunic of chain mail (or leather), and a circular shield. His favorite weapons were an iron sword, battle axe, long spear, and bow.

## JAPANESE ARMOR

The development of oriental arms and armor followed a different course from that in the West. Japanese armor was intended to terrify and intimidate the enemy as much as to protect its wearer. The favored form was a type known as scale armor, made by lacing together overlapping metal or leather plates, often lacquered. Helmets were fitted with wide, splayed neck guards.

## LONGBOWS & CROSSBOWS

Although the longbow was the favored weapon of attack in battle because it had a longer range and was faster to fire than the crossbow, the latter was favored by castle defenders because it was more deadly at close range. The crossbow had to be pulled back (usually by a winding mechanism) and fired a bolt (about 1 ft. long). Both weapons were preferred to early guns, which were dangerous and unreliable.

A longbow

A crossbow

An early medieval cannon

# The Age of the Gun

**P**robably no other single event has had so profound an effect upon the practice of warfare, or society, for that matter, than the invention of gunpowder and the subsequent development of guns. Weapons and warfare changed very little for much of human history, relying almost solely on sharp-edged hand weapons. The development of European firearms a mere 600 years ago, however, changed all that with a subsequent and dramatic increase in loss of life sustained during armed conflicts. Although the Chinese have usually been credited with the invention of gunpowder, some doubt has now been cast on this. There are several other claimants, including India and Arabia. Certainly, its full potential was not recognized until European scientists invented the gun, probably in the late 13th century.

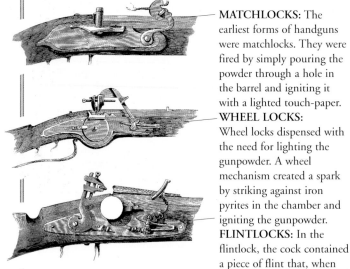

## THE DEVELOPMENT OF HANDGUNS

Early guns were unreliable and accidents were common. If too much powder was introduced or flaws appeared in their metal barrels, the guns were likely to explode. Artillery was a new and inexact science. The foremost problem was how to ignite the powder without the need to carry a lighted touch-paper.

**MATCHLOCKS:** The earliest forms of handguns were matchlocks. They were fired by simply pouring the powder through a hole in the barrel and igniting it with a lighted touch-paper.

**WHEEL LOCKS:** Wheel locks dispensed with the need for lighting the gunpowder. A wheel mechanism created a spark by striking against iron pyrites in the chamber and igniting the gunpowder.

**FLINTLOCKS:** In the flintlock, the cock contained a piece of flint that, when triggered, hit against the metal hammer, creating a spark. By simultaneously exposing the gunpowder chamber, the powder was ignited.

## THE FIRST GUNS

No one knows who actually invented the gun. All that can be said with certainty is that the first European illustration of a gun can be dated to 1326. No explanation is given, so we must assume that guns were already commonplace and had been around for some years before that. Early guns were vase shaped, but after about 1350 the more familiar hollow-tube shape made of wrought iron (shown here) began to appear, mounted on wooden supports. Projectiles were usually arrows or stone balls.

## GUNPOWDER

Although the Chinese have been credited with inventing gunpowder (about 1045), what seems more likely is that several researchers in both Europe and Asia were working on similar formulas simultaneously. Either way, the full potential of gunpowder was not realized until the late 12th/early 13th centuries, when the first guns appeared. Its early use in China had been confined to making fireworks or creating large explosions to frighten an enemy (as seen here) or to blast open a gate of an enemy city.

## FRIAR BACON

Roger Bacon (c. 1214–92) was an English Franciscan friar who was, in many ways, ahead of his time. A scholar and scientist, he was very conscious of the superstitious times in which he lived and wrote down the results of his experiments in code to avoid persecution. Whether or not Friar Bacon was carrying out his own independent research is not clear. What is certain is that he was the first person to write down the formula (c. 1250) so that gunpowder could be manufactured to a consistent standard.

## THE END OF AN ERA

Although the development of firearms has often been credited with sounding the death knell of the medieval castle, this was not the case. Early guns were neither reliable nor powerful enough to have much effect on stout castle walls. By the time guns were capable of causing substantial damage to stone walls, the day of the medieval castle had already passed.

A number of castles were either built, or altered, to accommodate guns, usually small handguns. The most common method was to change the more traditional cross-shaped arrow loop to one resembling a keyhole shape, as shown here. The gun barrel was passed through the circular hole while the gunner used the slot as a sighting line.

# The Development of Firearms

Following the initial discovery of gunpowder, it was some time before anyone had the idea of using the explosive power of the substance to propel an object and use it as a weapon of war. Early guns were fired by placing the powder and shot down the length of the barrel and ramming down hard. This method was known as muzzle loading. Accidents were common and the method was time-consuming, particularly dangerous for soldiers when under fire in the heat of battle. It soon became obvious that it would be quicker and easier to load a gun from the breech, or firing end, but this would necessitate a second opening into the barrel that had to be closed securely somehow at the moment of fire to prevent mishaps.

## ARMOR PIERCING

World War II saw the rapid advance and development of tanks and multigun fighter planes. Gun sizes on tanks increased from 40 mm at the beginning of the war to a powerful 88 mm by the end of the conflict. Mounted on swivelling turrets, first developed for the use of guns on warships, such tanks became incredibly versatile and could pierce 3 inches of armor plating at 1,000 yards. The example shown here is an American Sherman tank.

## BREECH-LOADING HANDGUNS

Although breech-loading cannons appeared probably as early as the 14th century, safe, breech-loading handguns were not successfully introduced until the early 18th century. The obvious dangers were the risk of burning or explosion in the face of the firer if the chamber were not properly sealed. The first breech-loading rifle appeared in 1812 but did not come into general service until 1848.

## NEW LINES OF DEFENSE

The introduction of artillery had a profound effect upon the design of fortifications. To begin with, guns were simply accommodated in medieval castles by adapting arrow loops for the purpose, but as guns became more reliable and powerful new types of defenses had to be designed to accommodate the new, larger guns and to protect against the effects of cannon fire. Medieval castles, which were already in decline by the 15th century, presented too large a target for gunners. Forts built after 1500 were low to the ground with massive earthen embankments behind the walls to lessen the impact of incoming fire. The old-style battlements were replaced with deeply splayed embrasures with circular or pointed bastions to deflect shot and give the guns maximum field of fire.

## AUTOMATIC GUNS

The development of automatic guns became possible after the introduction of metal cartridges. The first machine gun, or rapid-firing gun, was patented by an American, Dr. Richard Gatling, in 1862. It employed several barrels that rotated in turn. In 1883 the design of machine guns was revolutionized by Hiram S. Maxim, another American. His single-barrelled gun utilized the recoil action, which was used to load, fire, and eject simultaneously. The gun was cooled by a water jacket covering the barrel and was capable of firing up to 650 rounds a minute.

## BOMBARDS

By the mid-15th century, cannonmakers were beginning to perfect their art. They produced guns that were both more reliable and less likely to explode and of a much larger size. They were usually cast in bronze or, more commonly, wrought iron, consisting of separate iron tubes, held together with iron hoops. The largest cannons were known as bombards and some reached huge proportions, up to 18 ft. long (5.5 m), 18 tons in weight, with a caliber of 25 in. (63.5 cm).

## FIXED BAYONETS

Until the development of rapid-firing and repeating guns, when an enemy approached too closely, soldiers had to resort to old-fashioned hand-to-hand fighting. Often infantrymen, until the end of the 19th century, still carried swords and most had a bayonet, a kind of detachable spearhead, that was fixed to the end of a rifle.

## HOW THE WEST WAS WON

It has often been claimed that guns were responsible for European's ability to overrun the American Indians. While this is undoubtedly true, it is only part of the story, for what really "won the West" was the development of automatic weapons, capable of firing several rounds of ammunition without reloading. The first hand-operated revolver appeared in 1818 and in 1836 Samuel Colt patented a percussion revolver with an automatically revolving chamber.

# Military Leaders of the Past

Throughout history there have been a handful of military leaders whose deeds and exploits set them apart from all others. Most were generals who led their armies in the conquest of other lands. Included among these are Alexander the Great, who extended Greek civilization in the 4th century B.C. into Asia and Egypt. Rulers such as Alexander and Julius Caesar were intent not just upon conquest but also on the expansion of their civilizations. By contrast, the ruthless Mongolian leader Genghis Khan desired only power and exploitation. Other great leaders arose in trying to defend their homelands from invasion, as with Hannibal, the brilliant Carthaginian general, and Boudicca, the Celtic British queen, both of whom tried to halt the advances of Roman armies.

## ALEXANDER THE GREAT (356–323 B.C.)

Alexander the Great inherited his father's kingdom of Macedonia when just 20 years old. An inspired leader, he always led his army with his elite cavalry, the Companions. By 323 B.C., when he died prematurely of fever, he had extended his rule, and Greek culture, to Persia (now Iran), Egypt, Anatolia, and India.

## GENGHIS KHAN (c. 1162–1227)

In the 13th century, the Mongols established one of the largest empires ever known, extending over most of China, southern Russia, much of eastern Europe, and Anatolia. The empire was centered on Mongolia and its most powerful and ruthless ruler was Genghis Khan. He was a cruel man whose name roughly translates to "ruler of all men." He is believed to have been responsible for millions of deaths.

## GEORGE WASHINGTON (1732–99)

George Washington was born in Virginia and fought for the British in the French and Indian wars of 1754–63. An honest man, his integrity inspired his fellow Americans. He spoke out against British rule and, as commander of the colonies' Revolutionary Army, led the revolution for independence, becoming the first president of the newly founded United States of America in 1789.

## HANNIBAL (247–183 B.C.)

Rome's second attempt to invade Carthage, a city in North Africa, was thwarted by Hannibal (commander of its army in Spain) in the Second Punic War (218–202 B.C.). He marched his army, together with 40 African war elephants, around North Africa, crossed to Spain, and proceeded to cross the Alps into Italy and strike Rome from the north. He defeated the Romans at Cannae in 216 B.C., but was eventually beaten in 202 B.C.

## THE DUKE OF WELLINGTON (1769–1852)

Arthur Wellesley, 1st Duke of Wellington, was born of English aristocracy in Ireland and began his distinguished career as a soldier. He quickly rose through the ranks, but is best remembered for defeating Napoleon Bonaparte at Waterloo in 1815. He returned home a hero and entered politics, becoming Prime Minister in 1828. He was the first leader to also be Commander-in-Chief of the British Army since Cromwell.

## NAPOLEON I (1769–1821)

Napoleon Bonaparte was a French ruler and military leader of rare military genius with plans for world domination, who is said to have inspired Hitler. War broke out between Britain and France in 1793 and resumed again in 1803, after a short truce. Napoleon won resounding victories in Italy (1796), The Netherlands (1797), Austria (1805), Prussia (1806), and Russia (1807). A charismatic man, he inspired his troops by looking after their well-being and ensuring they were well fed. He was eventually defeated by a combined allied army and spent the remainder of his life in exile.

## JULIUS CAESAR (c. 100–44 B.C.)

Julius Caesar began his career in Roman politics and rose to the rank of general in the Roman army. He conquered Gaul and invaded Britain (in 55 and 54 B.C., respectively). He was later ordered by the Senate to disband the army but invaded Italy instead. Rome had been a republic, ruled by elected statesmen, but Caesar became power-hungry and wanted to rule alone, as emperor. He became dictator from 49 B.C. on. It was feared that he was becoming too powerful, which led to his assassination on March 15, 44 B.C. by his fellow politicians. He was deified after his death, with later Roman emperors assuming the title Caesar in his honor.

# Warfare Since the Middle Ages

The English Civil War
of 1642–49 was fought
between Royalists (known
as Cavaliers) and
Parliamentarians (the
Roundheads). It was
the result of many years
of conflict between
the monarchy and
parliament in deciding
who should rule the
country. In February
1645 Parliament created a
revolutionary military
system, the New Model
Army. Nationally
organized and trained,
and regularly paid, it
dispensed with the need
for mercenaries.

**A**lthough we now often adopt the somewhat complacent view that bloody warfare belongs to the Middle Ages, the truth is that, not only has mankind never been free of war, the worst conflicts have occurred in modern times, particularly in terms of casualties. Casualties in wars used to be confined mostly to those involved in the actual fighting, because of the hand-to-hand nature of the weapons used. The development of firearms and, more particularly, impersonal weapons such as bombs, which can inflict harm upon an enemy across great distances, has meant that civilian casualties are now very much a part of modern warfare, whereas before they were comparatively rare. Although it might sound absurd, in the past there was a kind of code of war. Today it is very much more impersonal with death and destruction inflicted by remote control.

### CHANGING
### STRATEGIES

Before the full potential
of gunpowder was
realized, with the
development of
firearms, its explosive
properties were used to
good effect in blasting
the walls and gates of
fortifications.

## AMERICAN CIVIL WAR

The American Civil War was fought between eleven southern states (the Confederates) and the northern (Union) states between 1861 and 1865. The resulting conflict was a particularly bloody encounter. A scorched-earth policy by the Union soldiers resulted in many Confederate families being left homeless. Civilian and military prisoners were crammed into "concentration camps," where many died of disease. Short of men, money, and supplies, the Confederacy was eventually forced to surrender.

## CHARGE OF THE LIGHT BRIGADE

The infamous "Charge of the Light Brigade," which took place during the Crimean War, fought between France, Britain, and Russia in 1854–56, was one of Britain's worst military disasters. Confused orders and incompetent officers resulted in a lightly armed cavalry charge straight toward the massed Russian guns. Strategists were forced to rethink their methods of attack as a result of such catastrophes.

## SAMURAI WARRIORS

Samurai warriors were an elite caste of bodyguards employed by noblemen in medieval Japan. They followed a very strict code and treated their swords with an almost religious reverence. It was said that, once drawn, their swords, which were two-handed with slightly curved blades, could not be sheathed again until they had drawn blood. The Japanese martial art of Kendo uses the traditional swords and face masks once used by Samurai warriors.

## AERIAL ATTACK

Professor Eduard von Eberhard developed the first effective antiaircraft gun for the German armaments firm, Krupps, in 1916, by utilizing the decreased air resistance in the upper atmosphere. It had a very long barrel and was capable of firing a shell a distance of over 60 miles.

# Attack & Defense

## THE GREAT WALL OF CHINA

The Great Wall of China is the only man-made feature on Earth that can be seen from outer space. It was ordered to be built by Emperor Shih Huangdi in c. 214 B.C. to keep out the nomads to the north of China. Maintained and rebuilt several times since then, most of this massive construction, which runs for 1,500 miles (2,400 km), dates from the 15th to 16th centuries A.D.

The twin principles of attack and defense have always gone hand-in-hand. Every advance in new methods of attack was met by a corresponding advance in defensive techniques. History demonstrates this pendulum swing throughout the ages, where first one side gained the advantage, only to be almost immediately outmaneuvered by the other. Nowhere is this better illustrated than in medieval siege warfare, as the series of illustrations on these two pages show. While no expense was spared in the development of new military technology and weaponry, defenses became evermore impregnable. The ingenuity of the human mind seems somehow to excel when faced with the problems of attack and counterattack, inspired by the basic instinct of survival. Many of the most significant advances in science and technology first began as part of a military strategy. The most spectacular example of this in the modern world, perhaps, is the development of the rocket, originating with the "flying bombs" made by German scientists during World War II.

## SIEGE TOWERS

There were many ways in which a fortress might be attacked. Archers could fire at defenders on the walls from behind wooden screens to give covering fire while others attempted to gain entry by scaling ladders or from the protection of a belfry. A belfry was a wooden tower that could be wheeled into position against the wall and then a drawbridge lowered from its top stage onto the wall top giving attackers direct access to the walls. However, ladders could be easily pushed away and belfries were susceptible to fire.

## SIEGE ENGINES

There were a number of different siege engines to help attackers gain entry to a fortress, some so powerful that they remained in use long after the advent of guns. The mangonel (left) was a huge stone-throwing machine, similar to a catapult. Others were the ballista, a kind of giant crossbow, and the trebuchet, which resembled an enormous sling.

## DEFENDING THE WALLS

Despite their bristling array of walls, towers, and other defenses, most castles were seldom called upon to withstand a siege. Their very presence acted as a deterrent and the outcome of confrontations was often decided by negotiation rather than by force. Sieges could last up to a year or longer but were very costly. Most defenders surrendered when faced with disease or starvation.

## JAPANESE CASTLES

Castles built in Japan and other oriental countries resemble, to western eyes, huge houses or temples and show few outward signs of being defensible. They were much stronger than they might first appear, however, with the living apartments ranged in tiers above a massive, featureless stone plinth that gave an attacker few opportunities to gain access. This view shows the 16th century Hiniesu Castle in Japan (Castle of the White Heron).

## AGE-OLD METHODS

Methods of siege warfare changed little over the centuries and most of the siege engines described here were used by the Romans and even the ancient Greeks. Often the defenders inside a fortress also had their own siege engines to shower the attackers with stones or burning straw. They fired a variety of missiles, including stones, burning faggots, shrapnel, or even dead horses to induce disease. Trebuchets could hurl a boulder weighing several hundred pounds a distance of some hundreds of yards and could reduce a wall to rubble with concentrated fire.

## SHRAPNEL BOMBS

The Chinese, although credited with its invention, were slow to realize the potential of gunpowder. Until the 15th century they confined its use to scaring away the enemy with loud explosions. They did, however, develop exploding shrapnel bombs, which they hurled among the enemy using traditional siege engines.

17

## THE FIRST SEA BATTLE

Although ships had been a feature of many battles, the Battle of Sluys in 1340 is generally regarded as the first true naval battle of modern warfare. Edward III defeated the French navy during the 100 Years' War and established English supremacy of the Channel. There is some evidence to suggest that guns were mounted on board some of the ships, making this the first use of firepower in a naval conflict.

## THE BATTLE OF JUTLAND

The Battle of Jutland was the only great sea battle of World War I. It took place on May 31, 1916, off the Danish coast between the British Grand Fleet, consisting of 24 battleships, and the German navy. Although the Germans claimed victory, they were unable to force a way through the British fleet and remained hemmed in for the remainder of the war.

## UNDERWATER ATTACK

Prior to 1900, submarines were used mostly for reconnaissance work, but afterward, once fitted with torpedo tubes, they became a very real threat to shipping. The electrically powered *Holland*, shown here, was launched in 1897 and, three years later, was put into general service in the U.S. Navy.

# Battles at Sea

*T*he control of waterways has always been an essential part of warfare. For the most part, in the ancient world, ships were used to transport men, equipment, and supplies, and not as fighting vessels. The Greeks, however, used triremes, rowed by citizen sailors, to ram enemy ships. After Romans first constructed a navy in their wars with Carthage, ships were used as fighting platforms for soldiers. Even up to the 16th century, when cannons, were mounted on ships, the guns were used to disable a ship so that the soldiers could overrun the crew; ships were expensive to build and it was considered better to capture and repair an enemy ship rather than sink it.

## BATTLE OF TRAFALGAR

Admiral Horatio Nelson (1758–1805) won a decisive naval victory against the French at Cape Trafalgar in 1805, confirming Britain as the foremost naval power in Europe. British warships at that time could fire a broadside every 90 seconds, twice as fast as any of their opponents.

# World War I (1914–1918)

The underlying causes of the First World War were complex and, even now, are not entirely understood. At that time, most of the major European countries were busy acquiring colonies around the world. The leaders of each country mistrusted the others and so a series of alliances were drawn up to achieve an even balance of power and prevent any one country from becoming too powerful. The spark that began the conflict occurred in 1914 when the heir to the Austrian throne, Archduke Franz Ferdinand, was assassinated. The Austrians blamed the Serbians and declared war on them. Russia went to Serbia's aid and Germany to Austria's. Germany had already been undergoing an armament program and began to flex its muscles, initially to establish itself as the dominant power in Europe with little thought of an ongoing international conflict. However, when Germany invaded Belgium, which had been neutral until then, a threat was posed to Britain's maritime security and so Britain entered the war. Soon after, the conflict escalated into a worldwide conflict.

## AMERICA ENTERS THE WAR

In the early stages of the war, German U-boats observed the international code of not sinking ships on sight without warning. In February 1917 they ceased to do so, which threatened American shipping in the Atlantic. America had been supplying the allies and was forced to enter the conflict. Germany had hoped to defeat Britain before the U.S. could mobilize its strength, but seriously miscalculated events. Germany formally surrendered on November 11, 1918 and signed armistice agreements dictated by the allies.

## GAS ATTACKS

When the war reached a stalemate position in the trenches, desperate measures were introduced to win the upper hand, including showering the enemy with poisonous gas canisters, such as mustard gas, which was a powerful irritant and caused severe burning. Soldiers had to wear cumbersome respirator masks as protection. Many died or suffered life-long respiratory problems as a result of even brief exposure to such gases.

Lettre d'un "Poilu"

Sans cesse, too papa, ma fille bien-aimée,
Baise ta chère image, en mon âme enfermée.

## CIVILIAN ARMY

The allied army consisted largely of untrained civilians and was initially no match for the German army. Britain, like other countries in Europe, had become complacent, and was unprepared when war was declared. Rising unemployment throughout Europe, however, meant that there was no shortage of volunteers, but there were serious shortages of materials, especially munitions. Women were forced to work in factories, shipyards, and even the armed services to help with the war effort in all the allied countries.

## AERIAL WARFARE

World War I saw the first successful use of prolonged aerial attack in an armed conflict. Machine guns were mounted above the cockpits and bombs were dropped over the side, taking the fight beyond the range of land-based or ship-based guns. Airplanes were also used to spy on enemy positions.

## DEATH IN THE TRENCHES

Following the military deadlock after the Battle of the Somme, both sides dug themselves into trenches. Life in the trenches was inhospitable, wet, and cold, and caused the war to drag on far longer than the six weeks most had expected the conflict to last. Complicated tunnels and dugouts were constructed with each side periodically going "over the top" to attack the enemy lines under constant fire. Loss of life was horrendously high for very little strategic gain and many of those who survived suffered ill-health for the remainder of their lives.

## MASS DESTRUCTION

For the first time in history, during World War I, the mass destruction of entire communities became possible, largely as a result of the massive new guns then being manufactured. Heavy guns, with a range of up to 60 miles, could bombard towns from a safe distance. Despite this, the basic tactics of the generals in World War I were the same as they had always been, in ranging armies in front of each other. The power of the weapons used, however, resulted in much higher casualty figures. Over 10 million people lost their lives in the conflict.

## TANK WARFARE

Armored cars had been used since at least 1904. But the idea of completely encasing guns in heavily armored vehicles driven on caterpillar treads and able to traverse any terrain was developed by a British Royal Engineer, Lt. Colonel Ernest Swinton. They were first used on the Somme in 1916 and then at the Battle of Cambrai the following year.

# World War II (1939–1945)

Although the reasons surrounding the outbreak of World War I were complex and are, even now, unclear, the reasons for the outbreak of the Second World War are much easier to explain and grew directly out of unresolved issues at the end of the first world conflict. From a military point of view, many lessons had been learned from World War I. In that war enemy troops still lined up in front of one another, in the time-honored tradition, to "shoot it out." Battles in World War II were much more tactical and relied heavily on the increased use of technology and weapons of mass destruction. This war has been the bloodiest conflict in history thus far.

Altogether, some 40 million people lost their lives, including many civilians and 6 million Jews who were persecuted by the Germans and deliberately put to death in "concentration camps."

## THE BLITZ

Having failed to defeat the British Air Force, Hitler continued his invasion plans by subjecting Britain to nightly bombing raids, both to destroy strategic targets and demoralize the civilian population. London was particularly badly hit, as were other city centers throughout the world, including Dresden in Germany.

## GENERAL ROMMEL (1891–1944)

General Erwin Rommel was one of Hitler's leading generals in the early part of the war commanding Germany's highly successful tank corps. His defeat at El Alamein in north Africa, in 1942, is generally considered to be a turning point in the war.

## AMERICA JOINS THE WAR

Japan joined forces with Germany and Italy, extending the war to much of Asia. Initially, America helped supply the allies against the Germans but was drawn directly into the conflict on December 7, 1941, when the Japanese launched an unprovoked attack on the U.S. fleet at Pearl Harbor, in Hawaii.

## SUICIDE MISSIONS

Japanese soldiers had a reputation for fanaticism and would lay down their lives for their emperor rather than surrender or be shot. The *kamikaze* pilots shown here were specially trained for suicide missions to crash their planes, loaded with explosives, into the heart of the enemy. The word kamikaze means "divine wind."

## D-DAY LANDINGS

The allies began their decisive push back against the Germans on June 6, 1944, with the reinvasion of France along the Normandy coast, known as "Operation Overlord." The Channel coast had been made impregnable by the Germans with a chain of fortifications. A British invention called "Mulberries," or floating harbors, made the invasion possible. All told, some 5,000 ships transported over 300,000 men, 54,000 vehicles, and 100,000 tons of supplies across the Channel, protected overhead by some 10,000 airplanes. Within a year the war in Europe was over (May 8, 1945), followed 3 months later by the end of hostilities in southeast Asia.

## BATTLE OF BRITAIN

In July 1940, shortly after France had fallen to the Germans, Hitler launched *Operation Sealion*, the code name for his intended invasion of Britain. For the invasion to succeed, however, Hitler needed to establish air supremacy, so he threw the full might of the German airforce, the Luftwaffe, against Britain. For over 2 months an aerial battle (the Battle of Britain) was fought out in the skies above southeast England. It was the first major battle in history to be fought solely in the air. Losses were heavy, but the British Spitfires and Hurricanes eventually won over the German Messerschmitt 109s (shown left), preventing the invasion.

# Military Leaders of the 20th Century

## MAO TSE-TUNG (1893–1976)

Mao Tse-tung was a revolutionary Chinese leader and founder of the Chinese Communist Party (1921). When the Communists broke from the Chinese Nationalists in 1927, civil war broke out. He inspired an almost fanatical zeal among his followers and initiated a cultural revolution, making promises of social equality. He became president of the People's Republic of China from 1949 to 1959.

**W**hereas many of the leaders of the past have led their country to victory during campaigns of aggression, many of the greatest leaders of modern times have come to prominence more for their inspired resistance to aggressors, answering their nation's call during its hour of greatest need. A notable exception was Adolf Hitler (1889–1945) who received fanatical devotion from his followers. However, the scale of atrocities during World War II prevents us from calling him an "inspired" leader when the memories and consequences of that conflict are still too close in time.

## EISENHOWER (1890–1969)

Dwight David Eisenhower (Ike) was a distinguished general in World War II, who afterward went on to become the 34th U.S. President in 1952. He was the Supreme Commander of the Allied Forces in the 1944 invasion of Europe and also of N.A.T.O. forces in Europe after the war. He developed a personal approach to leadership that made him seem less remote to his troops.

## SIR WINSTON CHURCHILL (1874–1965)

Considered by many to be one of the world's greatest wartime leaders, Winston Churchill (shown far left) succeeded in uniting the people of Britain and boosting morale when all seemed lost during the early years of World War II. A great orator, his rousing radio speeches lifted the spirits of an all-but-defeated nation. He became a Conservative member of Parliament in 1900, joined the Liberals in 1904, and reverted to the Tories in 1929. He became Prime Minister of a coalition government in Britain during the Second World War. In 1963 he was granted honorary U.S. citizenship.

### GANDHI (1869–1948)

Not all great leaders came from a military background. Some, like Mohandas ("Mahatma") Gandhi, preferred a more peaceful resolution to human rights problems. An Indian nationalist leader, Gandhi spent 21 years campaigning for equal rights for Indians in South Africa. He advocated a policy of nonviolent civil disobedience against British rule in India, which, from a military perspective, was difficult to contain. He was a leading figure in securing India's eventual independence in 1947.

### NELSON MANDELA (b. 1918)

Nelson Mandela joined the African National Congress in 1944, beginning his career as a black nationalist leader in South Africa. He campaigned avidly for a free, multiracial and democratic society in South Africa. Imprisoned between 1964 and 1990 he became a political martyr, continuing to inspire the cause from his prison cell. He was eventually released following worldwide opposition to his imprisonment and was elected the first black president of South Africa in 1994.

### "STORMIN' NORMAN"

U.S. General Norman Schwarzkopf (nicknamed "Stormin' Norman") led the United Nations' attack on Iraq in the Gulf War of 1990–91. In August 1990 Saddam Hussein, leader of Iraq, invaded neighboring Kuwait when talks about oil quotas broke down. The United Nations imposed sanctions on Iraq followed by a short high-tech war, which was all over by April 1991. Schwarzkopf's raid on Iraq, in the final stages of the war, is said to have been inspired by Hannibal's attack on Rome (see pages 12–13).

### GENERAL PATTON (1885–1945)

Like other great U.S. leaders, General George Smith Patton believed that personal contact with his troops was essential for good morale. His most noteworthy campaign was in 1944–45, when he led the 7th Army across France and Germany following the D-Day landings.

## STAR WARS

Both American and Soviet satellite technology was based on the enormous advances in rocketry made by German scientists during World War II, when the V2 rocket was developed. The first communications satellite, Sputnik I, was successfully put into orbit by the Soviets in 1957. Today, our skies are littered with several hundred communications satellites to aid the spread of information technology via computers, an essential part of modern missile warfare. The Strategic Defensive Initiative ("Star Wars") was a proposed system of orbiting space stations to detect and launch guided missiles.

## AERIAL RECONNAISSANCE

One of the earliest uses to which both cameras and airplanes were put was to take aerial photographs of enemy positions. Developed during World War I, by the time of the Second World War a whole branch of the military was engaged in interpreting the details of aerial photographs to follow troop movements and pinpoint bombing targets.

## ELITE FORCE

Throughout history elite specialist forces have been employed to carry out specific missions, mostly in secret, and often used during peace time when a government might not want to be linked to certain sensitive operations. Britain's Special Air Services (the S.A.S.) are an example of this (a member of the S.A.S. is shown here). The U.S. Green Berets are generally regarded as one of the finest and most effective of these. Training is rigorous and only those capable of survival in the toughest conditions are selected.

## THE U.S. MARINES

Only the best and toughest troops are selected for the U.S. Marine Corps. Personnel are trained in many military skills, including air, sea, and land tactics, and are capable of survival when dropped behind enemy lines. They are often the expeditionary force sent in to first engage an enemy and clear the way for the main military thrust to follow and as such usually face the fiercest opposition.

# Special Forces & Espionage

**A**rmies have always used spies to gain advance notice of an enemy's plans. Espionage was a particular feature of the "Cold War" between the West and the Soviet Union, when both sides rearmed after World War II, and continues to flourish in today's world of sophisticated information technology. One of the most effective methods of secret warfare is for a small group of individuals to adopt guerrilla tactics against an enemy. The Boers used them against Britain in 1899–1902 and against the Japanese during World War II. Its most effective employment in modern times, however, was by the North Vietnamese and Viet Cong against the French. Later, Americans were forced to adopt a strategy of defoliating the jungle to remove the guerrillas' cover.

## ATTACK BY REMOTE CONTROL

A whole range of cruise missiles now exists, including the nuclear-armed Tomahawk, which can be launched from the ground, or from aircraft, submarines, or warships, and directed by sophisticated computers to their targets. The Patriot missile (shown left) is a highly advanced mobile battlefield SAM (Surface-to-Air-Missile) system. It uses phased array radar for accurate target detection at several hundred miles and employs antijamming devices to avoid destruction.

## EARLY WARNING SYSTEMS

The first advance warning system to detect approaching aircraft was *radar* (Radio Detection And Ranging). It was invented in 1935 by Robert Watson-Watt and worked by transmitting radio waves and then scanning the returning echoes to measure the distance and position of the reflecting object. It was fitted to the Boeing B-17 Flying Fortress bomber, making it the first "self-defending" airplane. The system has been greatly advanced since then. The jet shown here has been specially adapted to carry an AWACS system (Airborne Warning And Control System). It carries long-range surveillance and detection radar with C3 (Command, Communication, and Control) facilities to detect friendly aircraft, in addition to several other sophisticated tracking devices.

## GUERRILLA WARFARE

When faced with the superior forces of a more powerful enemy, the smaller military forces of a nationalist or revolutionary movement often resort to guerrilla tactics. By dividing and isolating the enemy and making lightning strikes when least expected, such fighters can often create stalemate situations or even defeat a superior enemy. Guerrilla movements also have the added advantage of being able to mobilize the local population against the common enemy and to conceal themselves among them. From such a vantage point they can strike right at the heart of an enemy with sudden acts of harassment or terrorism.

# Attack from the Air

## AIRSHIPS

Airships (known as Zeppelins after their designer, Ferdinand Graf Zeppelin) were huge, gas-filled dirigibles ("blimps"), but with a fuselage structure beneath the skin. They were cigar-shaped, with tail fins; an engine was mounted in a cockpit suspended beneath, making them surprisingly maneuverable. First invented in 1900, they were used during World War I by dropping bombs over the side.

Anew form of attack emerged during World War I: attack from the air, which has since become a major feature of modern warfare. From an early date, guns were mounted on the flimsy new biplanes, but bombs were also dropped over the side of the cockpit. More commonly, however, bombs were dropped from huge airships ("blimps"), protected by fighter planes. Since the Second World War, aerial tactics have mostly been in the form of massed bombing raids (or, in modern times, the use of "Smart" bombs, which can pinpoint a target more accurately) to destroy strategic targets and significantly reduce an enemy's firepower before sending in ground troops.

## STEALTH

"Stealth" is the popular name given to the technologies that enable aircraft, missiles, or ships to avoid detection, either visually or by radar, sonar, or infrared sensors, thus making them virtually undetectable. Most commonly associated with aircraft, the Lockheed F-117A Nighthawk Stealth fighter and the Stealth bomber (shown above) make an unforgettable sight, with their sleek black lines almost invisible to the human eye, even at close range.

## FIGHTER ACES

Before interrupter gear was developed, which enabled fighter pilots to fire through the blades of the propeller, many biplanes in World War I had a machine gun mounted above the propeller, which made it difficult to aim. Nevertheless, the war saw several fighter aces, including the Frenchman Georges-Marie Guynemer (shown here) who claimed to have shot down 53 German planes.

## BOMBS AWAY

Before the advent of rockets and guided missiles, the dropping of bombs from aircraft was very much a hit-or-miss affair. It was difficult to be accurate and pinpoint a specific target from great heights. One solution was to employ massed bombing raids to obliterate an area, thus increasing the chances of hitting a strategic target. When the allies began their daring daylight raids on Germany in the closing stages of World War II, the Americans lost an incredible 4,750 B-17 bombers.

## JET FIGHTERS

The jet engine was developed in Britain in 1937 by Frank Whittle. Although not used extensively in World War II, both Britain (with the Gloster Meteor) and Germany (with the Messerschmitt Me 262) had jet fighters in service by 1944. The first jet-to-jet combat took place in 1950 when the U.S. Lockheed F-80C Shooting Star shot down a Soviet-built MiG 15 during the Korean War. The high-speed jets shown here are U.S. F-15C Eagles.

## HELICOPTERS

Although the principle had been understood since 1907, the first helicopter with a powered rotor, the R-4, was developed by Igor Sikorsky (a Russian-American) in 1939. The first use of a helicopter for troop transportation in combat was in 1951, by the U.S. 1st Marines during the Korean War. Helicopters have an obvious advantage over fighter planes in being able to take off and land vertically in difficult terrain, and in their greater maneuverability. Attack helicopters are mostly used to launch missiles, such as the McDonnell-Douglas 530 MG Defender, shown here, with missile launchers located on either side of the fuselage.

## SUPERIOR MACHINES

The main fighter plane used by Germany at the time of the Battle of Britain was the Messerschmitt 109, which was equipped with a central cannon. The British Spitfires and Hurricanes were equipped (at that time) with eight Browning machine guns mounted in the wings (so interrupter gear was unnecessary), capable of delivering 9,600 rounds a minute. This, coupled with their greater maneuverability, gave the British planes an obvious advantage over those of the Germans.

# Modern Weapons & Warfare

**S**ince the end of hostilities in the Second World War there have been well over 100 major conflicts in some 70 countries worldwide. Many of these have been localized disputes, in underdeveloped regions of the world, but several have been potentially inflammatory and could have led to worldwide conflicts. Following the end of the Second World War, an arms race began between the United States (and her Western allies) and the Soviet Union. Each side acquired sufficient nuclear weapons to destroy the world several times over. Arms agreements were eventually reached in the 1980s and 1990s and many warheads were disarmed, but since then several other countries have acquired weapons of mass destruction putting the world under constant threat of nuclear attack. Another feature of modern warfare has been the development of biological warfare, where warheads containing lethal containers of bacteria can be released on an unsuspecting civilian population.

## KOREAN WAR

In 1910 Korea was annexed by Japan. When Japan surrendered at the end of World War II, Soviet troops occupied North Korea and American troops occupied South Korea. In 1950 the Communist North Koreans, backed by the Chinese and the Soviets, invaded South Korea, which was aided by the United Nations, whose army was under U.S. command. Open hostilities ended in 1953, but all attempts to unite the two factions have failed and they remain divided.

## GUIDED MISSILES

The idea of exploding rockets was first used by the Chinese as early as 1232. The first guided missile was launched in 1917, an automatically piloted biplane called "Bug" SSM. During World War II, German scientists perfected the V1 and V2 pilotless "flying bombs." Once launched, the engines were timed to run for a set period of time before they fell and exploded on impact. Modern computer technology means that missiles can select a target with pinpoint accuracy.

## GULF WAR

On August 2, 1990, Saddam Hussein, president of Iraq, invaded neighboring Kuwait, rich in oil revenues. The United Nations imposed economic sanctions on Iraq and on November 29 issued a resolution authorizing the use of military force to liberate Kuwait. Hussein had been stockpiling weapons and many feared a long, protracted war, but what followed was a brief, high-tech war resulting in an allied victory, headed by the United States and Britain. The war began with a series of massive air strikes to limit the effectiveness of Iraq's ground forces, using several guided missiles that had never been tested in armed conflict before.

## A NEW FORCE

Modern military forces are better equipped with weapons of destruction than any of their predecessors. Weapons of devastating capability can be launched from vast distances. Although "Smart" weapons can avoid hitting unnecessary targets, modern neutron bombs are now capable of emitting short-wave radiation that affect people but leave buildings still standing.

## ATOMIC POWER

The scientists who developed the atomic bombs that were dropped on Japan, bringing World War II to a close, were Germans who had fled the Nazi regime and found sanctuary in the United States. The first generation of atom bombs used a combination of conventional explosives to drive together elements of Uranium 235 to produce a chain reaction among the neutrons. From these, scientists developed hydrogen bombs, which were more powerful than atomic bombs. Nowadays, a whole range of devastatingly powerful nuclear weapons is available to add to the armories of military powers.

When Japan continued to fight after the surrender of Germany, drastic action was thought necessary to avoid invasion. It was decided to drop two atomic bombs on Japanese cities, Hiroshima and Nagasaki (bottom right). So devastating was the destruction that both cities were virtually razed to the ground and people still suffer the effects of radiation. Japan surrendered almost immediately, on August 14, 1945. The picture above shows a nuclear bomb test on the Bikini Atoll in the Pacific in 1954, with the typical mushroom-shaped cloud.

## VIETNAM WAR

Civil war broke out in Vietnam in 1954 between the Communist-backed north and the United States-backed south. The north used guerrilla warfare, using the jungle as a refuge. The Americans responded with a scorched-earth policy of deforestation, but it proved ineffective. American troops were gradually withdrawn between 1969 and 1973 in response to public pressure. Two years later South Vietnam surrendered to communist rule.

# DID YOU KNOW?

**That croissants were invented to commemorate a siege?** Although usually thought of as French, croissants were first made by Austrian bakers. In 1683 the Turks laid siege to Vienna and began tunnelling beneath the city walls. Bakers, working through the night to make bread, heard the tunnellers and raised an alarm, thus saving the city. Viennese bakers devised the croissant (based on the crescent moon symbol on the Turkish flag) to commemorate the event.

**That Navajo Indians speak a secret language?** During World War II Navajo Indians were employed by the U.S. government to pass secret military messages in code using their native tongue. The unwritten Navajo language is practically indecipherable to anyone who does not speak it and it was used as the basis for a cryptic code that neither the Germans nor the Japanese were ever able to crack.

**That rockets provided the first airmail service?** Although more commonly associated with warfare and, in modern times, space travel, early rocket pioneers experimented with many other uses to which this invention might be put. In 1928 the Austrian engineer Friedrich Schmiedl experimented with rockets that had hollow nose cones, containing mail, that separated in flight at a prescribed distance and parachuted to Earth. The experiments were continued in Scotland in the 1930s by Gerhard Zucker to deliver airmail to the islands. Despite some success, the experiments were abandoned.

**How French cuisine came about?** French cuisine is today famed the world over for its variety and creativeness, but did you know it first came about as a result of a siege? In 1870–71 the Prussians laid siege to Paris, cutting off all its food supplies. People were forced to eat horses, cats, dogs, frogs, rats, and even animals from the zoo in order to survive. To disguise the taste, cooks devised all manner of unusual sauces and recipes to make the food palatable.

**That bombs can bounce?** During World War II it became necessary to destroy strategic dams in Germany. The British inventor Barnes Wallis devised bouncing bombs that would skim across the water like flat stones until they hit the dam wall, whereupon they sank to the required depth and exploded. The shock waves collapsed the dams.

**That Hitler was a secret believer in the occult?** In the Hofburg Museum in Vienna is a spear, called the Longinus Spear after a Roman centurion who owned it. It is reputed to be the one that pierced Christ's side as he hung on the cross. The spear assumed occult significance as a lucky talisman and was said to bring victory to anyone who owned it. Past owners included Constantine the Great and Emperor Charlemagne. Hitler, who was very interested in the occult, acquired it and had it placed in a vault at Nuremberg Castle. Shortly after its discovery by American troops in 1945, Hitler is supposed to have committed suicide.

## ACKNOWLEDGMENTS

We would like to thank: Graham Rich and Peter Done, for their assistance.
Picture research by Image select.

First Edition for the United States, Canada, and the Philippines published by Barron's Educational Series, Inc., 1998

First published in Great Britain in 1998 by ticktock Publishing Ltd., The Office, The Square, Hadlow, Kent, TN11 0DD, United Kingdom

Copyright ©1998 ticktock Publishing Ltd.

All inquiries should be addressed to: Barron's Educational Series, Inc.
250 Wireless Boulevard, Hauppauge, New York 11788
http://www.barronseduc.com

Library of Congress Catalog Card No. 98-70735

International Standard Book Number 0-7641-0534-5

Printed in Hong Kong

Picture Credits: t=top, b=bottom, c=center, l=left, r=right

AFP/Corbis-Bettman; 30l. AKG; 2br, 5cr, 12/13cb, OFC & 13cr, 13t, 12cb, 15tl, 17bl, 17tl, 16tl, 18/19, 22bl, 23tr, OFC & 24/25c, 25c, 25br, 24bl, 27br, 26c, 29tl, 30bl, 28tl, 31br, 31tr. Ancient Art & Architecture; 2/3c, 2tl, 3tr, 5tl, 5br, 6bl, OFC & 6/7c, 6tl, OBC & 6c, 8/9cb, 13br, 17tr. Ann Ronan @ Image Select; 3br, 2bl, 5tr, 4/5c, 4/5cb, 7br, OBC & 9tr, 8bl, 11tr, 10/11cb, 10cl, 10bl, 11bl, 14br, 14bl, 16bl, 16br, 18c, 28bl. Chris Fairclough/Image Select; OFC & 10tl, 14tl, 28/29b. Corbis-Bettman; OBC & 4l, OBC & 15r, 26br, 31br, 32c. et archive; 18tr, 18tl. Courtesy of Fine Art Photographic Library; 15c. Giraudon (Paris); IFC/1, OBC & 2/3cb, 17br, 20bl, 21r, OBC & 20tl, 21br(x2). Hulton Getty; OBC & 23b, 22b. Image Select; OFC & 7tr, 9br, 11br, 12tl, 12/13ct, 21t, 20br, 22tl, 23l, 24tl, 25tr, 29br, 31c, 30/31cb. Mary Evans; 8/9ct. Pix; 24bl. Quadrant Picture Library; 27tr, 29t. Rex Features London; 26r, OFC & 26tl, OFC & 28/29c, 30/31ct. Sipa Press (Paris); 27cl.

Every effort has been made to trace the copyright holders and we apologize in advance for any unintentional omissions.
We would be pleased to insert the appropriate acknowledgment in any subsequent edition of this publication.

BARRON'S